I was diagnosed with paranoid schizophrenia in late August 2010. I have since had many different psychoses, weaving in and out of them with this disability, becoming clear and then foggy and then tortured and then once more clear again. During these psychoses, I feel much more wolf than human, and many times have taken my bottled up confusion and frustration out on the poetry page. Parts I and IV of this book were written in Spring of 2016, and Parts II and III were written in early August 2010 after nearly a year of undiagnosed mental hell. All these poems are the original, unedited versions.

-Sam Caton

Table

PRELUDE

It opened. Slowly at first, carefully, projecting. Saddened by its own speed and the speed of its surroundings. The Muses watched, slowly at first, carefully, projecting.

Thus they sang:

"Forever, sing. Forever, laugh. Forever, be. Songs in sweeping, songs in motion, songs in delight and gifted tongues, forever. Forever, sing. Forever, laugh. Live forever."

He heard the songs as the crevices cracked and skewered. He heard the songs, and he sang. He laughed. And he was. He sang songs in sweeping motion, songs of fright and songs gifted in rhythm.

First it was a dream, nothing more.

PART I: Waxing Gibbous

Theorem I

The Living seek to devour The Dead.

whereas: The Living fear The Dead because there is no map made after death that can be read by The Living. (point A)

whereas: The Living are jealous of The Dead because death transcends pain. (point B)

whereas: When The Dead are devoured by The Living, The Living have The Dead inside of them and The Dead have life surrounding them.

1) Why do The Living want The Dead inside them?
   a) It gives the illusion that The Living are the masters of Death. (ref. point A)
2) Why do The Living want to surround The Dead?
   a) It is an attempt to raise The Dead. (ref. point B)

The Living seek to devour The Dead.

CONFLICTION

My mental illness does not define me, no, but still-
It rips me apart.
The endless desire guards this accursed ego.
The mutated delusion rapes my subconscious.
And the correlation between light and dark finds new ways to disintegrate my
mind, acid upon acid, layered in a blessed home that is no haven from the
billowing smoke clouds corrupt, kindled with a spark of tested blossoms, of
tested blossoms matriarchal, invoked and tribal. Call me to the wind, ever
humming like blue caverns of triangular eyes, three to look upon death and
three to bow in eyelid respect. Night approaches always. The snow-lipped
hills barter the cost, losing only to themselves in an ambiguous oscillation, this
forgiven circle of terrible thought that means nothing to those who do not see
from emotion outward.
I am conflicted.
You are conflicted.
Ghosts linger on, linger and sway to the searing heat from a fire built not for
light but for an oracle, not for heat but for eloquence, for when the concrete
does not exist, the abstract must do.
The skies are clear above where they are not clear. The ground is damp but it
needs to be.
We build our belief, we build the evidence we use to believe, and we build the
faith that the invisible exists because everything we see does not satisfy our
feeding minds. Constellations guide us, but not of stars. Of thoughts,
connected reaching emotional conflicting.
Desire, how you've destroyed me.
Desire, how you've kept me alive.
To isolate is to shave this head.
Do you see the trees? Do you see those weathered companions wise,
wandering in grateful pinion edification? They see you, they see you and shed
a tear, a conflicted tear that rips out their heart at the same time as strumming
the stringed harp holy in peace, in progress, in a wild stallion saluting the
lonesome prairie and running because that's what he wants to do.
And still we wander, willows looming with dripped saltwater inaugurations.
Emptiness leads to the choice of what to use to fill.

There is truth in the undergrowth.

There is truth in the hollow logs decaying in the calm entropy of redefined nourishment.

There is truth in the hawk perched precariously upon rocks of lattice lordship, profane and sacred simultaneously.

There is truth in the happy brook healing the mossy stones sprinkled delicately upon the underground's canopy.

There is truth.

We just need to find it.

And then the choice of what to fill ourselves with can be made.

Shall we search? Shall we discard this banal map, the plebeian course constructed by minds that are not our own, that do not command these fingers as I begin to write, that do not command our wolfhound hearts that mourn freedom's falsification by light of a moon that understands and speaks in whisper, quiet, so quiet, so calm in its care as it brightens the wooded path twisting in this mental wilderness?

DO YOU SEE?

Shall we open these three eyes to a dawn of inescapable rumination, lost and found and bladed like the grass on a hillside of yesterday's swirling confusion? This life is all it needs to be.

We already are the canyons of crystallized harmony, the pyramid in the sun, the molecules ignited to a forest fire of plausibility, etched within oak and pine and bound by the specter of a self-aware talisman.

Open.

The cliffs draw near, and as the water pours I see a beast approaching, a beast of string-tied illusions, a beast of hallucinogenic plants morphing like autumn oxytocin, retracted to a ladle of abstractions lifting the liquid to heights beyond these hands, beyond the diamond portcullis sliding upwards and backwards and inside out.

Your.

Does the curse need to be lifted? Does Hecate's empty palm suggest a doom that draws itself upon papyrus tender and bold and crawling throughout the reeds towards a crocodile invocation? There is a unity in our spines. There is an earthquake in our thighs. There is a pattern in our thoughts, nebulous and aged.

Eyes.

This volcano is overdue.

This path is made by animals and lead by animals and followed by animals. There are no humans amongst the silhouettes.

This trail has not been forgotten because it has not been known. It has not been remembered because it has not been known. We are these aching branches.

HERE

So adorn this grandiose delusion with feathers, with garments made from sapphire selection and stability. These worlds were never yours. These wars were never owned by you or anyone else and result from nothing but a canine trying to protect their owner trying to protect their canine.

If explode we must, then let us do it in a blaze of unprecedented love, a deluge of uplifting words validating as the vines that hang from trees like hair that doesn't need to be combed. The tangles are natural, you see, and unimportant except for the fact that they derive from nature.

Eat with me.

Drink with me.

We haven't long.

So this sweet separation between landmass and island construes itself to be itself and nothing more. Nothing more than the buzz of a hummingbird's wing beaten to the sound of the quietest drum that readies the time and rhythm, the pollen precious and clandestine, the whir of the blades encompassing all over thought through pruned bushes and wild lilacs and the notion that every place has its time and every moment is defined by the place that surrounds it.

Be here now.

Be here, and choose.

You can decide whether or not this moment is special, whether or not it is a treasure trove trodden upon and hidden by dirt lobbed from a shovel indifferent. Unearth me, my coffin, my bones. Breathe air into this vigil that sings that elusive joyful dirge, for when the circle ends the circle begins again.

A new mind.

A new body to dedicate.

A new animal arisen to tread upon leaves fallen from elm trees aloft, guiding its steps in gracious disclosure, whispering the seedling truths upon ears ready and eager and forgiven.

TAKE A WALK

There is a man, a dark man, shadowed and leaning up traced walls willful, passive in dichotomy and as red as the blood that drips downwards spiralizing and stern. This man visits only the insane, and visits only in moments of sanity.

And so I took a walk. I placed one foot in front of the other and watched the yellow leaves tumble like autumn's treachery, giving in to the frigid blusters that pander at our Western hearts, that train us for time.

This natural anxiety is a result of distance. It's a result of caring to reach, to extend these tired arms to the treetops in order to find the sun, for yes, this forest is dark.

As dark as the man that approaches. Slow is his gait, deliberate, mindful. He says nearly nothing, and his round eyes show a world within a world. A universe of catapulted disarray, destitute for coins but as rich as he needs to be.

And so I took a walk, the ferns and lilacs lingering upon my nostrils as I wade through the fond flora that finds us naked, naked and yearning and apprehensive. This broken tongue finds solace in the humming meadows, the whistling wind rallying Gaia's parapets deep into the mammoth hills, the gargantuan mountains voluptuous like a pair of lips longing to be kissed.

It's a blessing that we don't have to live forever, and if we do, through some strange glitch in the system, I feel a shift will be made to make the infinite endurable.

The man draws near.

His quiet kitten scampers nearby, darting into bushes of salvia divinorum and coming clean in order to break through to the bricks of humanity's completion. These glass walls will not hold us.

I am your mirror, and you are mine.

There is so much to say but there is no way to say it except through riddles, and when there is no answer to the riddle the riddle sways like truth and becomes an entity unto itself, a thought that stands alone on a grazed hillside of perfect complexion.

This vast unknown lingering upon our tongues beautifies the storms, complements the rain as it plummets North and South and East and, as always, West so deep. Listen as the water falls.

It's funny, isn't it? These whirlwinds we create for ourselves and then long to leave, to go back to boredom until, in all our wisdom, the whirlwind begins once again because of the boredom we previously reverted to?

I take a walk.

The man approaches. His pace has quickened like the sand we stand upon. His black hair shines with grease and with a golden crown that symbolizes a kingship of nothing; no color on the flag waved: launched and trapezoid.

This banner is white but not of surrender. Its colorless haze shows a fealty to nothing, not even neutrality because neutrality suggests realm.

Is it possible to not be a citizen? Native, yes, but not of origin?

His cat purrs gently, contentedly, giving fidelity to its own black fur and the dead mouse lovingly wrapped within the blanket of the feline's jaws.

The man stops. He bends down. He pets the cat.

Walk with me.

THE HAUNTING

She's always there, but she isn't the one waiting.

This bandolier grows heavy, heavy and charged with electric drug-infused lullabies, lingering upon my tongue as I attempt to ignore her presence. This shadow has shifted. This image, burned in my mind, becomes itself and in doing so becomes myself.

I am the one waiting.

Eager.

Eager.

Eager for sleep, for the end to come, for the secrets to be revealed and then in a loving embrace death finds us all wanting not.

The woman with a million faces follows still, singing the siren's song in my seclusion and laughing her shining laughter at my self-induced plight.

We are already here, you and I. We have arrived at the present and we are safe from the past. The future will never reach us and a transcendental reversion to beliefs not worth believing but certainly not worth forgetting continues to bring me back.

A wheel, a wheel that spins.

A flower that grows in the desert.

The luminous voice of the disembodied sweetly comforting the lost soul that I am and have been and will be.

And so the dream occurred, restless wanderings of DMT blossoming into the night sky, into a red dress dancing and the face of the faceless that laughs into the star's golden light. "Follow me," she whispers. And so I follow. "Take me where I need to be. I am not lost in body but in soul."

Waiting.

The vision dominates and disintegrates the lilac brain latched behind these ocular closings. The drug of death defied seeping into a shadow that revitalizes the search.

To search you must know what you are looking for.

To search you must have have eyes, eyes un-gouged and ready.

And to have these working pupils, my hair must remain long, long as the river that rolls inside hearts to lakes inside souls. There are monsters in these lakes, sleeping monsters that will wake when the time is ripe and right and realized upon multitudes to multitudes.

Shackles bind these eyes, I do not know of whom to look upon. These vines wrapped lovingly around my biceps bind me tight to this mast, and as the rain and sun and nutrients reach the ship's bow the vines become stronger.

Can I truly curse this vine? It keeps me safe, safe from the icy plunge of prodigal and heedless incarceration.

As long as I am in a cell, let me be with this kind plant.

Eager.

Eager and frightened.

And yet there is comfort calling, sliding into my sideways mind sending thoughts of heedless love, heedless forgiveness, heedless faith, faith that I do not own but instead receive.

She is not the one waiting.

She is the mystery I cannot solve.

I am the one waiting.

It started with a song, melodious incantations pervading the dark osmosis of psychotic mist. The song lifted and carried me, teaching the thoughts to connect with one another.

Excitement was due.

Love does exist, and it is patient with my slow growth.

She is not the one waiting. She is the one singing.

The lyrical constellations guided the journey from slumber to a bladed awareness, from a calm to a chaos, but not one of weather, instead of confusion in peace, confusion in presence, confusion in waiting and in what to wait for.

It is better to feel a ghost that loves you than to be alone in the vast, naked, frozen stiff for even when the winter wind blows you whisper in my eager ears and tell me "Wait. Wait a little longer. Have patience. You are loved."

Nymph, you are my tumor.

Malignant.

Fearsome.

Forgiving in all my humanity and faltering swords and divergence from the trail that leads to our connection; a connection that may never be but still you are with me as I walk and pet this content kitten in grace that the mutilations of the mouse gives life.

And as the clock spins, the signs continue.

Another clue, another dive into confusion.

This spirit knows no bounds, fallow ground surrounding the garden, delaying the garden, these legs are not open because they are invisible and if I can ever see the invisible my fear will overcome my ability to consummate.

And at the times when you draw back, when you hide from my piercing gaze that sees nothing but feels everything, I long for your haunting words to once again reach my ears through the thousand tongues singing, the million voices and faces representing who you are and what you stand for and why you follow me.

Confliction.

Confliction and fear.

My beautiful phantom, I cannot define you, but, in peace, be not far from these aching bones.

I will wait.

PART II: Full Moon

Theorem II

To Live is to Desire. To Die is to transcend Desire.

whereas: Desire is the longing of the flesh, mind, and heart.

whereas: Longing is rooted in the fear of going without.

whereas: Death forces contentment of the flesh, mind, and heart, regardless of availability through escaping the body, the brain, and the soul.

whereas: The embrace of Death now satisfies all Longing, and Longing remains as a pail with a hole in the bottom until Life reaches reckoning.

whereas: Life leads to Death as Longing leads to Fulfillment.

To Live is to Desire. To Die is to transcend Desire.

1) insanity

Tied to an airplane
Explaining brevity
Disgust
A bum smokes a cigar on the sideways train track. Twenty new numbers pilfer
his imagined brain like a
horde of pigeons. Mushy feet, smelly skin and clothes wrinkled ignore the
numbers, twenty ten and
twelve fold. A cow sits the sideline silently, sweating from a sweltered
morphine shot. No udder. This
one's male.
Tied to the jet, the clipped quail wings compute biscuits and canned salmon.
Explained, the newcomer bum finishes his lazily inhalations and dies, smelly
clothes and skin.
Disgusted, the pigeons and cow jump over the moon.
The cursing elder blames the weather. The child, smart and sure, blames God.
The workingman blames
his job. "Quit, for fucks sake!" his wife shrews. "Well, I need it."
Blame the God of the child, blame the entertainment of God with the elder,
blame the life breath of the
workingman and let his wife blame him.
Humanity is tired. Bustled, fro and to, tampering sick feelers masticate like
moldy chicken pox, the
ointment cools. Crush demarcation, crush the cursers, crush the cow and its
damn friendly pigeons.
Humanity is lonely and tired, try to not sleep, too auger sucked and mediocre.
Lewd lilies of the field
eventually quit blaming anything but blame itself. Installing hooks and levers
and bells, whistling
thoughts dreary with oval remedies, machinist modernizing medical
masterminds build nothing but an
ugly old woman with a cane and a bad attitude.
Utensils, twenty new numbers and a bad fucking attitude.
Immaculate mused and infectious, ivory welders and ingenuity. At least he's
creative.

Punish the greedy baby. Beat the elder's face in with words.
Hand grenade the house, watch the rubble rise and the tentacle tantrum precision bewilder the
televised appeal. "Come one, come all, watch for free! Insanity as entertainment!"
At least he's creative.
Envision the tug of a wire. Let it cut through the skin. Keep hesitating. Stop. Stop. Think. What does
that mean? Where is he going with this? Is it sad, offensive or both? Stop. Go fuck yourself. Come
back. Don't be offended. Feel the wire?
The circus is in town. The clown is dead. Insanity as entertainment.
"Quit, for fucks sake!"
"Well, I need it."
Happiness is a dog that follows us around. Sadness is a dog that follows happiness. At least he's
creative.
The wire tugs.
Rudeness tip toes snickering the snide, imagery angers and retaliates. Wander the cobblestoned cliff
dwellings, eat Navajo bread, this peyote ghoulish and ancient and mysterious. Everyone is mysterious.
Serenity finds herself as eager as ever, let's be calm and collected, shall we? The only things that matter
are the things we care about. If you don't care about something, then why should it matter? If
something doesn't affect you, then why the hell would you care about it? That's the polecat's point of view, the smelly skunk hobbling through trash receptacles and shit. Feed
off the dump. It works and takes next to none. Feel threatened? Spray the motherfucker! Make him smell bad! That's his problem.
Blame the skunk and his godless odor, stinky bastard got me wet.

2) dandelion stew

Feel the tug?
The lawmakers only care about one rule: don't break the law.
Illicit weed growth, don't water weeds, pluck and pull. That's the name of the game. Chop liver and
slice the stew meat snatched solemnly, yuletide expanse now governs the lawmakers. Let's build this
man.
Colonial in thought, walk the plank panic struck and stricken by a lightning bolt. The clouds make it. The
clouds are water, smash water together and die. Anarchy ensues in the mind. We are the mind, the
brain has no god but the brain itself. We worship our thoughts.
At least he's creative.
What isn't masturbation these days?
Banjo strumming, blowing your nose. Get on the remote control and go surfing from dawn and
breakfast till an oil dripped salad, a prayer, two beers, a pill and a pillow. Talk a walk. Exercise. Go to
the bank, clear important shit up. Put on deodorant. We're people, for God's sake, not skunks.
What isn't masturbation these days?
Read a book, a story, a place and a time and a person and a thing. An idea. Be the noun you are. You
might as well. Go ahead, the lawmakers know the game. Go to work too, yes, do that. Take the bus
downtown, get dropped off. A baseball game, a midnight snack, a newspaper explaining the world, a
blue shirt, a green shirt, a pair of jeans bought with work, a new toy. Thank the brain it's Christmas!
Keep beating off.
Prepare for your future, clip your toenails and brush your hair, pour soap into a wet box and make your
underwear smell nice, get lunch with a friend. He'll have the number 3 while you take the number 4

with a side order of fried shit. Pick a hobby. Start a collection, build it, and destroy it for a few bucks
and a memory. Go to church. Socialize, eat a meal, take a shit and a nap.
What isn't masturbation these days?
Swear with your buddies, play a game, go to the mall and watch people pace indecisively. Pretend you
know who you are, pretend other people care who you are, make a joke and laugh. Be kind, be funny,
be serious. Touch your dick. Pray. Walk into a building, purchase an animal, take it to the building you
own, name it, feed it, punish it, play with it, put it down. Let it be your voiceless, sexless, thoughtless
child. Brag about it. Use its company. Teach it a trick. Show a dear friend. Bury it.
The lawmakers have their own pets. The gardener with his mute canine seamless and agnostic, quiet
harped elusive, what do these dogs think? Who's smarter, a dog or a toddler? A gnat told me a story.
"When I was young, the world decreed a day without masturbation. Everyone sat quietly on their asses,
no one said a word all day until a six year old asked for a cookie. The lawmakers buried him."
I told the gnat a story.
"When I was old, a six year old told me it was my fault. 'My fault for what?' I asked. 'For being old."

3) the damaged bandaid

Peeling it off the skin slowly stuck, the hairs prickled and clicked.
A cigarette, a butt, a garbage can. Join the crusted band aid.
Sitting in the lawn breeds nothing but bent grass. Stare at the dirt. There are
insects at work. Edited
tractor smudges try to smile through a bridge too far, banish the band aid, burn
the infection, let the
searing fire cleanse. Is that medical? Does it follow procedure?
The moles are destroying the lawn, delving dire dirt deep in caverns, twisted
lairs confused and
treacherous. Set the mole trap. We don't want piles of dirt on the lawn. The
lawn isn't dirt. Don't pile
dirt on dirt. Kill the foolish mole with a portcullis. Join the crusted band aid.
In rectifying the master plan, the procedure, who cares if it's medical or not?
Who cares, the mole is
dead. Now all we have to do is clean the dirt off the dirt.
Feel the tug?
Windy tunnels and dry ice. It's cold. Don't touch it. Put on your coat, put on
your hat, put on your
lambskin boots, enter the windy tunnel. Howling hoots of blustery blows,
shiver the spines, freeze the
tendons, turn white skin to red, burnt in a frozen smile. It's procedure, it's how
the coin tosses.
Animals live in their own houses, don't worry about them. Keep to the subject
matter at hand, please.
Throw the ice, let it join the crusted band aid.
As the lake becomes hard, the fish lose their ability to jump. They can't jump
inside the water. Only
from water to air is their jump a jump.
Chop the ice, catch the fish, chop its head.
Become fishers of men. What is the bait? How will we catch these men? And
what about women and
children? Are they out of season? Let's use love as bait. We'll throw them a
little love to tempt them,

let them bite it, and reel them as they fight the fisher. I had a one up close, next to the dock. I netted
the fucker, lifted him ashore. Two options. Which one is procedure?
It wasn't an easy choice for me. I could keep it or throw it back.
If I kept it, I would have to gut it, chop off its head, take care of all of the mess, bring it into my house,
cook it, and eat it.
If I threw it back, it would be back in the lake and I would be where I was in the start. It would be as if it
never happened. The fish swallowed the bait as I stood there deciding.
A cigarette, a butt, a garbage can.
A cup of coffee, a quick snack.
A beer. Might as well, they're sharp.
Back out to the dock my footsteps took me.
The fish escaped, it took my love back into the water. Carrying it in the stomach, digestion took its
course.
I stuck my hand in the bucket. No more bait.
Back to the dirt, the mole pile, scrounge around, bury the muzzle, sniff the scent in finding.
A cigarette, a butt, a garbage can.
Back to the dock.
At least he's creative. Join the crusted band aid.

4) complications

Paradox impersonations run hedgehogs, flattened by tires twirling. Poor little bitches. Cut tracings, old
man masterpieces paintings persnickety. Smear charcoal, shadow and shade, who needs color? Black
and white's pretty. Zebras, penguins, skunks, cows, dogs and cats and dogs. Lots of animals are black
and white. Not all though.
The complications whine. Catacomb lists, old grave whistling citations, different shapes of stone stuck
straight up, erect. Erect the symbolic holy death rock. Yes, yes, and carve the deceased name.
The complications whine and moan. Rugged limp limbs lounge lazily, people do what they want. Black
and white newspapers help them. "Do what you want by doing what we show you!" Those words
screamed incessant, headlines and headlines.
If I could ask God one question it would be this: "What is going to be the last headline of The New York
Times before the world ends?"
Things will be complicated then.
Tanks are tanks, warplanes have wings to fly. So they fly.
Baffled nebulas rumble. The bathroom needs cleaned, clean it. The trash is overflowing.
Whelps, baby otters, ducks and geese, thirty kinds of fish and counting.
Try polishing the padded windows with a map. Try cleaning what needs to be cleaned. If you don't, the
need doesn't disappear like memories. It stays put. Stammered, stammered and violet, the flowers
linger lowly, hanging their heads as shameful rain gravity knocks them wet.
Relic rusts, dry toothed umbrellas angle and oscillate. The brain beats blooming, don't fight it. Fight it!
Don't fight it. Fight, fight and emerge! Slayer stung the dratted snail shell, the manuscript of marching,

the manuscript of municipal court, the manuscript of hairy toes and the shaven armpit of a swimmer.

Don't jump in the water if you can't swim. Don't smile if you're not happy. Don't make a joke if you

don't want people to laugh at your words.

Complications are necessary for the simple, they are gelatin. They are gelatinous hazes of umbilical dots

connected. The food needs to get there, the nourishment is true and the vitamins are vital.

Teething baby otters, disrespectful geese and the two ducks doomed to walk into the mouth of lion.

It's okay. The cycle of life. Lions need protein.

So find the Amazon, go find it, go find the utilitarian ladle, drink from the soup flow and eat potatoes

ripe with a cannon blast.

Crumble down with the mountain, don't slide like a rock. Fall.

Plummet south, invariables voluptuous and vicariously accounted. Volume I, Volume I and II, Volume I,

II, and III: They're in a row, just like the ducks.

The ducks will walk into the mouth of a lion.

Bless the lion, bless the ducks, bless the amino acids.

Vanish among the mist particles, wear the cloak of nakedness and follow a sunspot, the explicit entity of

hellish delight, descript and vacant, vanish and impart.

Seven baby otters, six goslings and a trigger happy son of a bitch.

We are not usual.

Don't prescribe to me.

Nobody is common.

Don't prescribe to me. Feel the tug?

5) polishing feathers

Louder! Louder! Thinking loudly inside one's own head! Oh my God!
Never glower, paralyze the strumming radio chords, and bleed them dry in
cleft hangers.
A heron walked in the marsh. Strutting arrogance lost, left to right. Stabbing
the air with its narrow
beak, beating its head in motion.
Pleasant blasts tranquilize trauma, vouch and wail.
Are you upset? Does this upset you? Do you have words to say?
Frilled penchant bold and tethered, please knock before you enter. Knock three
times. Keep the
succession quick. Glare at the stuffy, noisy sun. Glare at it and wait for it to go
down. Heap the shit in
piles and let it sweat profusely, profoundly, prolong the wait, don't let
excitement mangle your meshed
desires.
Ignore the stupid heron. All he does is stand on one leg and wait for fish.
Deny the truth long enough for it to disappear. It's what everyone does, isn't
it? Maybe not. Probably
not. No. Who knows? If idle hands are the devil's workshop, how does the
devil accomplish anything?
Stay idle, stupid cunt devil. You won't get anything done with your hands.
Involuntarily dew sprouts like bean shoots shorn and fresh. Keep the beat. Still
four four.
Embrace eventually like a brother, say it's okay to be eventual, let events play
themselves instead of
taking action. What is taking action? Can you stop?
Sagged eyelids heave motorbike evacuation. This catches the sight, this brands
images into the brain.
Oh holy brain! Fuck the brain.
Jewelry wears itself, it's only another drug. Will the drug round the neck. Will
it to life. Maneuver
around the goatherd, the shepherd, the herd itself. Don't get lost among the
livestock. Pry the princely

demons awry with ashes and zapping eyelets methodical, mutilate the imp's heaving ribcage with a

screwdriver. Puncture a lung, reach into the garbage, pull out the damaged band aid and patch it up.

The lung is your tire. You lose a lung, you quit moving. You run out of cigarettes, you walk to the store

and buy more.

The heron's back. His blue back scattered in a white reclined druid's robe. Sing a song heron, sing a

tune for your little fish to hear.

The heron's words are forgettable at most:

"I'm passive, I'm nautical, igloo incarnations swell in my bird brain, I live inside my head just like

Humanity. I worship my brain. I hunt for these fish. I can fly, fly like relationships, as mucous

membrane contemplates itself, myself, me and my own prescription specific: fish. Retaliation of the

blasted demarcation, generous and knifelike and fatigued. I'm active, I'm of the air, my feathers dry

themselves with a windy towel. Navy, the bane of the land. Army, the bane of the sea. Fix the groove,

hinge the door, swing it wide with a belly full of dead fish, envision a tomorrow that doesn't involve

herons, and forget these words."

Stupid heron. At least he's creative.

Creation is here. It's still here. It's still happening; from noun and idea to verbal process.

A crablike nasty shot to the skull, it's happening still and we are blind.

Enamored with letters, aiding the future together in morbid honesty content, so how do we think

without using words? The animals must do it.

Talented, talented these animals must be.

6) the man I met in my brain

I met him on a muggy day congested. His airtight mix tape smelled panoramic
with levity and brevity,
brief mannered in musical time.
"Good morning, mystic, I'm in your head, I speak only to you and you can
barely hear me. I'm not real.
Neither are you. Feel the tug?"   ·
His soggy skin reeked of mule fur and orchestrated numerals, Roman and
void. Traction traced a cut, a
suture, slightly bloody and barely worth mentioning.
"Twelve proverbs, twelve proverbs, each it's own answer. Listen, you'll listen,
and question each trite."
His toothless grin morphed the words, glinted with saliva. Disgust. He spouted
his first three eagerly:
"Every man is given a choice between choosing and ignoring."
"A proverb requires wisdom and cannot deem itself."
"To preach is to choose, to ignore is to preach."
He paused politely, pressuring me to review his words.
His putrid face molded once again. The next three proverbs rang out.
"The wind is to the weather as the bird is to the feather."
"The brain is to the word as the wind is to the bird."
"The thought is to the person as the dialogue is to the character."
My mind, sore and shapeless and tired, belied up and floated. Laughing gas
and loud emphatic chests,
angry disarray, vanity smoldered shellfish that clicked and clacked together.
Hampered, immolated, styrofoam in nature, tiny little bubbles popping
together to build white
repudiation. Who is this motherfucker, putting these ideas into my mind? Why
can't I stop him?
The next three proverbs rang out.
"The stage is to the actor as the person is to the character."
"To relish in a pointless proverb is to seek an answer that's already been
given."
"To eat is to become the food you throw in the garbage can."
Depression hit me like a slug.

At least he's creative.

He barely hesitated before the final three proverbs ejaculated.

"Idiots choose to ignore. Wise men choose first, and then ignore."

"A worm to fish, a thought to interest."

"Do unto others what you would do to yourself if you were them."

The man in my brain disappeared, boldly going as he came, ignoring me and my contemplations.

Fuck the brain and its insistence.

Manage the nimble nuances next and next and next. Smell the flowers if you are close to them, smell

the fourth fingered panfish as it cooks cleverly.

Smell the grass that's been sliced in two.

Smell the empty wine glass.

Smell the garden estate.

Smell the sea salt ocean incarnate.

Smell the air, sniff.

Smell the cookery and the brass bell old.

Smell the matchbox struck and stricken.

7) the sparking

Melon rinds sit on the front porch, a knife digs into a piece of wood, a shaving joins its friends on the
ground. Ritalin carp and ugly catfish wander the air of the lake, ludicrous and lengthy, the orchestra
only breathes delinquently and daring.
Emulate the mogul, kill the mogul, and discard the mogul.
Everyone, let us become.
Let us bonfire blaze the magistrate to pieces, the third eye stabbed by cedars.
Revel in wondrous unity,
we are, we are. We will be and fume to pieces, produce molecules in life's wandering whale song.
The cello.
Hopeless and tired torn phantasm to jagged jungle directions imbedded.
Meager portions, darkness
drear and draped radiance entrenched, dung beetles quietly rolling the dice in patience. Impeccable
stars and vast overwhelmed yet tiny beetles slow spin the shit they find. Look at those fucked up bugs.
Why do they roll shit slowly? Speed it up.
The piano.
Now they aren't so serious, their heart rate has increased. Perilous creeps of nightlife languish in a
possum's head. The tail twined and wrapped rat-like hangs upside down.
Kindling the reveled
productivity, the anger incites.
Old elephant gun tactics, these ones.
Ancient, to say the least.
Meditate on modular post hangings, signs that say "Wanted: Dead or Dying."
A six pack, a delirium, a
pair of oven mitts used as boxing gloves bloodied.
Predominate navel cavities now integrate, desire the scent of machinery keys and envision seventy-two
times around a global jugular. Pause.
Reflect.

The wire hurts.

Basting a chicken on a Sunday morning, stab the dumb bird with a trident and a butcher knife. Tear

apart its flesh with your teeth, tear it to pieces. Moisten the morsel, swallow it and go to sleep. Wake

up from your bedridden nap, take a shit and wipe your holy ass. The dung beetles will take care of the

rest, cover your slippery tracks with rain.

Take notes! Yes, take notes! Put them in a place where you will remember to look at them.

Don't forget to read what you have already written.

If you do forget to read what you have already written, you will also forget what you have written.

Remember words.

Let the directions direct, you might as well, it isn't going to send you to Hell, is it?

Voodoo dolls build the bugler, build the ion instruction, build and raise the prodigious art magnifier and

study bullshit until you get paid for it.

A degree. A dynamo. A flaming set of drug addicted children hardly impaired enough to get bad grades.

A legend. A myth. A tale. Tell the tale, sing songs and laugh, languishing on your own specific tone deaf

chortle. Mathematics and arithmetic. Counting numbers. Do all this, it makes people happy.

Varnish the wood, paint a house blue, set your mortgage papers ablaze in a furious bout of masochistic

fantod. Remember the dreams you have at night. Tell them to people. They'll believe you.

They care, they do.

8) welts

A one-eyed dog, a marble allusion, and a barrel full of battery acid.
Stark raving insane the mad canine measures rudimentary thoughts.
Bludgeoned and broken,
ludicrously in love, mashed like a rotten tomato in fall's forgetfulness. Rather
than growl, sit. Rather
than bark, be quiet. Instead of running in circles, stay put. Rather than beautify,
muse yourself to sleep
with foolish hope.
Mellow and drained and fashionably late and over the so delicately put top.
Rekindle gliders on a Monday morning. Break your bread in half.
People, they're everywhere. They're all over the goddamn place. Who invited
everyone this time? Oh
it was so and so again. That's okay. Everyone's cool.
Laundry hampers overloaded erupt like a volcano. The clothes smell like shit.
Hold your breath while
you put on your shirt. Heave. Heave.
Creativity at its worst.
Snickering at the questionnaire, the slivered snot nose encompassed the
bullshit. Regulate that temper
of yours; don't be hurt by these words. Don't take them seriously. For God's
sake, what do they mean?
"I'm not as hurt as I am sad. I'm worried about you."
I already guessed that.
"How?"
Fuck, I don't know, I've been to Hell before.
"That's one way to put it I guess."
It has to be, I wrote it.
"Shit."
Move on from this self singled out snippet, decide what you are thinking.
"I don't know what to think, I'm reading this. You're the author."
How do you know?
How the Hell do you know?
How can you know if button boxed babes utilize an orca stereo? The whale
song, the whale song! They

hoot like horns. Like gigantic owls of the ocean. Climb a ladder evolved, make haste in ivory mushroom
clouds billowing and bantering and buying us time to keep reading.
How can you know if there is any truth whatsoever in a poem?
Execute him! Go ahead, who's stopping you?
Insanity as entertainment.
Polish off that stadium rule, toss the core into a whirlpool, watch the pool drain itself. Stave off that
stadium aristocracy, fuck the man and his sick bellied astrology, who put those lights in the sky? Not
you. Not I. Certainly not either one of us.
"That's a given."
Well good, it's a damn good thing I gave it to you then.
Veiled in blushed ignorance, this brained shithole of vomit spewed and spat has barely been tapped.
Beg the dog, teach it to beg by begging it to beg.
Teach the baby to make baby noises by imitating the baby noises the baby makes.
Teach the cat to shit in the litter box by shitting in the litter box. Use your left leg to paw aroma and
dust and dried piss and sand and chunky graveled feces over the wet stank of disease.

9) anonymous

Crude oil and peat bogs strand the stringy hair, slough slinking toads of thrill
seeking package peanuts
pick through their choices.
"What sick imagery will this one contain?"
Don't label me, bitch.
Elegance in aura enchanted, give a breath, please do, give a breath.
Go ahead, enjoy the juniper spine tingles, the fantastic tremble of true beauty.
Catch fireflies in radiant
music. Echo in the shouting pines, levitate the feeding mind from former chaos
and embrace natural
embodiment. Harpists play, strum the string sound.
A pony whinnies.
Cough up blood.
Exemplify the glade clusters, do this and that and the other.
Television sets, traffic lights, talking boxes with plugs. Charbroiled beef
bought with a butcher's dime
last Tuesday. Bottom's up, take a few shots.
Cough up blood.
A pony gets put down.
Surround nature itself with nature. Vie with your wrinkled eviction to another
prison cell. Hope it's not
the case, give a good word a good word or two. Slander the stork head thimble
runner, slander him and
dictate a new set of eyeballs revered. Prestigious they are, stampeding
borrowed ecstasy like a
downplayed doctorate degree duly denied of sadism and vile virtuoso.
Keep following these directions.
If you do indeed keep following, become you will, become and become.
The ant colony harmonious, the scraped sky forgives buildings majestic and
manmade mountain peaks
pointing. Clueless antagonists deliver mail, packages, anthrax stamped
serpents solidify the cultures
crumbling aesthetic and pathetic crutch-like dependence on shopping for
clothes.

Is art really that enjoyable?

What isn't art these days?

Retaliation, cause and effect, bacteria brainwashing thrice abruption, idioms incinerate as easily as

pocket lint. Shotgun! Did you call it? Can you sit beside the driver this time? That's the best seat.

Nanny yourself. Take time to take time. Relaxation is important. It helps appreciate relaxation.

Usher in Volume IV. It's coming, be patient.

Piety, respecting authority, pretention, a smile.

Alleviation as a badger, exemplifying morgues redeems the blistering heat.

Matriarchal despond abuses

gavel degradations, deliver us from evil because we don't know how to deliver ourselves.

Quill ink dipped and dunked, delude the Danish stories, kill Hamlet right off the bat, save us from

soliloquies stuffed with tedium and childlike indecision.

At least he's creative, poor bastard.

Fortuitous angel encounters, bladed and baffled and slick with yellow fever, eloquence gutted at its

zenith by sickly invocations and rehearsals and cognitive receptors corroded.

Bring the apocalyptic muse, appropriate magic's demise.

Can God above, He who created the earth's breath, He who made the dinosaurs, He who killed the

dinosaurs, He who invented the sphere, He who is running this terrible and inexplicable inertia towards

the inevitable, He who sets up and destroys, He who invented peace and pain and progress, can He do

magic? What is God? God is God. That is that.

Magic.

10) volume IV

A camel loses its round herd, runs out of its hump and disappears into the
desert to die.
A herd of camels.
The Sheik knows how to get water. Take an ice pick, thrust it into the camel's
hump and see the pretty
pink fountain embellish.
I met the Sheik on snowy summer morn, belayed by vivacious revelries and
costume parties. Sixteen
shots of pure iodine, a syringe full of dysentery and a six year old flogging
himself with a cat o' nine tails.
Goddamn kid, this isn't the fucking Inquisition, this isn't Wichita during
tornado season, this isn't gilded
chemicals uniting, this isn't insanity, you're fine; get your dick wet.
Get laid, get some action. This is about sex, not love.
The six year old met the elder again.
The six year old took thirty five brass tacks and pushed them into the elder's
sagging belly.
The elder asked him to.
The elder himself never counted sex as too high of a priority.
The last tack held a piece of paper with three clever reminders.
1) Always assume. Assume as much as you can. This way you won't ever be
surprised and you
won't be as stupidly unprepared as you might have been.
2) Keep ninety-nine percent of your assumptions to yourself unless there is
reason to spout. Don't
believe any of them until you can believe them without much assuming
whatsoever.
3) Always assume other people assume about you. Feel the wire?
Mental prostitution. Absentees and pork rinds, squelching those water proof
sandals in mud and decay.
Slithering boardwalks of ecstatic wood paths overwhelm; deer beaten and old.
Look for the deer. Spot
their spotted babies, their graceful does, their gallant antlered males dwelling
between the ears.

Say "Hello" to them. They're listening. They won't respond. Not often. Nearly never.

I talked to a stag one day. He told me a story brimming with arrogance. This is that the deer said:

"I was young, too brown and green behind the rabbit ears. I was walking my dog in a park, eating grass
and smelling clover. I came across a road sign. Deer crossing, that was the gist. Feeling safe and secure
and elegant and respected and calmed by the sign itself, I crossed. My dog walked behind me, his loyal
tail wagging and his soggy tongue panting. A car came, some rusty Buick covered in mud and shit and
dead bugs and their guts. I hopped into the ditch. My dog got flattened. I'm scared of people now. I
only like deer. I try to spend as much time as I can with my doe."

Listen to the pompous priest-like preaching this shivered beast has sung. Hear the vile medication of
jumpy wariness. His antlers remain sharp.

The six year old met this deer.

The six year old startled this deer.

The deer chased him away with his pointy horns.

11) the whale call

A small pail filled to the top:
Cartons and cartons of empty cigarettes, tobacco-less and bland:
Legumes without shells, a shock collar and twenty new numbers:
A nudist colony on the Fourth of July:
Blood blisters without a care in the world:
An extinct species of fish from Borneo:
A radio signal eating at the ear:
Impossibility searched and discovered:
Ten monks, ten arrows, nine graves:
A wounded monk blaming his credit card debt:
Inch worms outrunning snails:
An angry household guest expecting dental floss:
Whimpering nocturnal bugs amused:
Missionaries without a religion:
Quizzical reviewers hoping to gain:
Ventricles replaced by tinfoil and sheetrock:
The man who repairs the refrigerator, the woman who darns tattered clothing:
Iguanodons having tea and coffee on a deck:
Atlantis found, Atlantis lost:
Flint and tinder connections sucking the reader to decide:
Analogous whiffs of blasé encounters:
Pleasurable pocket derivatives:
Buddhism being wrong:
Tawny octopi appreciating the meticulous:
Vague attractions to the genius of Ingrid Bergman:
Fully furnished houses that are clean, big, and empty:
Marching in single file:
Yak fur in 102° weather:
Withered tulips nibbled by a small animal:
Palestinian rugs threaded with care:
Mediation:
A 12-gauge painting the air with brain matter:
Volume VIII:
Addictions to narcotics, food, and talking:

Millionaires trying to decide what to buy:

The poor man trying to decide how to survive:

A woman with three young children, an infant, a drunk husband, a burnt dinner, a sore tit, a fulltime job,

a messy house, a cavity, two separate grocery lists, a speeding ticket, an overdraft fee, a broken baby

monitor, six headaches, a missing set of car keys, a ringing phone, a missed appointment, a smelly trash

can, unshaven legs, a freshly dead pet, and exceedingly good manners to her customers at the fucked up

store where she works.

13) benign apparitions

Treachery! Treachery! The inhalations of a pattern he created has crumbled! Illustrations rapidly pillage immunity: don't underestimate the overture. Don't vivify an explicatory
bladed banister, the bottoms-up bequeathing of bolded bunched braids demoralized. Advantageous
and nefarious, noted by notoriety for a poker table prescribed; we verify modules as often as cattle shit.
Alluded, the illusion panics. The hawkeyed certain mesh, mix well! Mix well! The wreath immobilizes
itself, give parry! Give parry! Have faith in your true Love.
Hell bent at rebuking the catechism, freedom itself had self proving to do.
An ostrich searching for its egg, a doctor looking up a word he forgot, a lackluster baron bursting with
stickles and droves of mild weather belligerent, they all add up. Add it up yourself, add up the bullshit.
Add up the cattle shit to see numbers and numbers, equations and equations and equations.
Tyranny! Tyranny! The escape pod has a code! Forget the code and blow up in the acid possessed
space ship.
Go to space and explode yourself.
Mattocks and pesticides, wigged out and barely self enough to have thorough awareness.
Mental explosion. Frightening polyester tapestry twined, LSD injection in the wrists, in the eyes, in the
ears, in the brain, in the tongue, and in the nose. The spring springs, shot and shooting, the body
twisted and morphed, on the edge.
Wide eyed, the vision: a drug trip.
Seething and obnoxiously fucked up, a bruising disruption.
Treat him like a babe! Give him a book to read! Pretend you are him and when he makes a decision you
consider wise, compliment him by complimenting yourself! When he takes a hint and acts like a baby,

tell the arrogant sick motherfucker to grow up and get some fucking balls!
Evacuation. Mirrored Mistoffelees and an insightful knack for pretending
you're dumb as fuck around
people.
Plagiarism methodic, venue palindromes and a wishy washy kind hearted
crowd appeal. Flip the shit on
their heads, turn the tables a bit. Put them on the edge of their seats,
excitement is a goddamn must.
Improvised articulation, maddened hornets, vague alleviations, a razor sharp
butter knife, put the ball in
their court for a bit. Toss a stinger or two their way, envision a demon
possessed manipulation, swallow
a few pebbles to break up the accursed process of breaking down a simple
meal.
Thank the stomach it knows what it's doing. Thank God you have a stomach.
Thank the food for being
edible and thank the brave scapegoat for not bowing down and giving planet
earth a blowjob.
Evoke remorse. Feel the remorse you provoked. Use it. Ride it. Ride that
horse. Ride that remorse
through the summer on Pluto.
Insolence! Insolence and a bad fucking attitude.
Tune in! Tune in! Turn your radio dials to hear the fucked up evil space baby
spout bullshit!
Go fuck yourself: Volume VIII.
With your cars, money, health bars, petroleum infused equestrians, rabid
machete wielding blasphemies
against love and its holy patience, anatomical prescriptions, mundane
fascinations with the mundane,
decrepit patronizations of the greedless, diluted absolutions, available
malevolence, cantankerous
retaliations at a red colored truth, trivial pollutions of megalomaniacal
bourgeoisie, and vindications of
the spirit's thirst. Go fuck yourself.

PART III: Waning Gibbous (The Song of the Birds)

Theorem III

The Living's truest Desire is to have knowledge of Death.

  whereas: Desire's roots come from the unknown.

  whereas: The truest unknown of The Living is Death, the construct and the verb.

  whereas: Once peering into Death, The Living Desire knowledge without actualization and faith without trial and error.

The Living's truest Desire is to have knowledge of Death.

Open

Your eyes, wired ecstasy definitely vacant hollow canopy. Blue, blue like
bodied water wet and winding river minding business, its own, blue. Aqua .
allocating every raiding winter wonder willow waiting patiently for weeping
wondrous tree to thunder, hovered hooves in plunders blunder, it starts with
nothing ends with nothing builds with everything destroying something that
catches leaves and breeze blown thieves, grievous wreaths of fire breathes.
Breathe in, breathe out, shout the sun and its light swindled oracles, lungs in
pairs, eyes in pairs, ears and feet and hand in pairs, two by two by two two
times. Sky blue, cindered second hand, chimney smoke slyly singled broken
cries in mingled horror, misery, ringing horror twisting me to bring the gore,
the red and orange, the bread of life, the water pours. To feed on time, to eat
the oceans blue bought rhymes and salted potions, emotion lingers in always,
forever wanders through our hallways, blue enchantment. Encamped lamp lit
destruction of the feeding mind.
I have no reason, nor do they, nor do you, to in life stay, except the reason of
pure logic, be it or not? That is the answer. In life we are caught.
Boiled eggs twine in DNA, string the world and spin it, hatch the hutch in
delinquent disgust, raise the noses to sniff up the air of arrogance. Start with a
mirror, end with a reflection, a direction, an inflection inflated with riddled
perfection, who are we to know or claim we can grow, to say without flow the
water remains. To smile like butter cut through a knife in strife we will strive
to the end of our life.
Blue lashed blinked, slinking the foxtail, the groove splintered dovetail in
peace and in love sail the boat, the goat, the saddle, the marriage of life and of
death must rattle our cages in orchid and rosebud perception, taming the
reflecting reflection's direction, perfecting the upward inflection, the theorem's
fear comes from love and its spiraled correction.
Bask in the sunlight, the family's delight, the trite joys of sleeping sound
through the night, if advice could be given by understood minds, then advice
no longer would be screamed towards the lines.
If God is love, then love to be worshipped.
Zombies stalk stingy chalk filled sidewalks. The living gawk and gander and
shoot and kill and live and gander and gawk they do still. Shrill is the sound,
the screech of an eagle. Empty the hoot of an owl. The seagull, it squawks in

annoyed annoyance they sing, the hummingbird's silence rings the beat of its wing. The crow it repulses, on shit it will feed, not picky or pretty, black honesty reads. A rooster will strut and wake in the morning, till cleavers fall cutting the brain and blood pouring from heart through the neck to the sphere of its head, lopped off by the farmer, the bird runs its circles, dead running and headless and bloody and red.

The brainless eagle, flying from mountains and craggy cliffs chopped by axes and by God. The Zombie, the Bird, the living they ponder and wonder why actions they see don't follow their God, their order, their contra fled border, their bricks and their mortar, the churches they build, their idols incarnate far from it to guild together to meld and weld with the feathers from headless birds flying, ignoring the weather.

If God is love, then love to be worshipped.

What

If love is God, then what are these idols, created to placate the simplest of titles. Complex, yes complex, not simple is love when God to be honored is peace like a dove, and fear, intense fear, the power of love, what power is power when God above sits and shits on the earth with love, bloody love, sick and twisted from start to redemption, it hovers harangued by a cost, what cost is the cost, when lost are we all from alpha to end, when maps cannot be made of places we can't go.

Pacing. Headless. Circles.

I met the Cartographer, he rarely disposes the Artist's invocation of roses and poses. To stand in a spot, so still, says the Model, to aid in the Artist's depictions, the novel. The Cartographer travels and draws the map, yes, but the Model must freeze and be frozen in place so by the Artist in accurate precision be traced. The ship, the eagle, the airplane in soaring continues on paths moving, ignoring The Cartographer's map, a rough sketch is all that indeed can be used in creating a path large or small. The Model is pictured. The Artist takes his time. The Cartographer in desperate plight tries to paint the Model, moving in flight, the eagle wings beaten like hummingbird spite. I met the Artist, he often complains of the Cartographer's pain, the battle to map out the travelling plains. "It's like standing in rain, and watching so quickly, a single raindrop falling fast from the cloud, not losing focus, staring straight on from the start to the finish; from cloud to the lawn." The Artist, he's honest, he's tired and true, taking time step by step to show what he drew. The Cartographer's lies cannot be untrue when impossible it is to map how he flew. The Model, he stands, in boredom respect, in bitterness baled like hay stacked to rest, waiting for fire from heaven or earth to consume his denial of changing his shirt.

The Cartographer, offended and angrily angered by the Artist's encampment on cliffs ripped asunder, challenged the painter, the singer's choice placement and asked him to wonder why.

"Why do you sit in hours and hours, still as the Model, painting the picture, singing the song, repeating the strokes until to perfection the painting is drawn?"

The Artist in patience and meticulous care, answered the Cartographer with a stare and a glare.

"The portrait, the meaning, the process my friend, its beauty slow going doesn't mean to offend."

The Model collapsed in hopeless fatigue falling from the cliffed rocks down into the sea.

"Look what you've done, you Artist, you fool, you've lost what you're painting through time and its duel."

The Artist, now angered, leaped up and proclaimed:

"A map! Dear Cartographer, of hills and of plains, of mountains and deserts, of plummeting rain, can you produce anything other than pain? Show me your progress, your process, your meaning, your portrait, its beauty, the directions so teeming, describe where you've been, the patterns in flight, the story of alpha to end of the night."

Little

Time stopped sudden, luck holding the Model's mouth closed barely before lungs inhaling drown. One hand outstretched from the sea, grasping at nothing except hope, paused by the frozen clocks, wet with salt and water and desperation. The Model, still living, clenched by the ocean, still dying, suspended in blue.

On the cliff's edge the Cartographer, holding his sketch, stands eye to eye mirrored with the Artist, the wretch.

The headless eagle, not bothered by time, flies down from the sky to sing its own rhyme. Perched on the Artist, paused like his brothers, the eagle screeched love while in time the frozen still hovered. The headless eagle, spouting his song, sang with blood fountain flowing from the cleaver stroke strong. Thus he sang:

"You three fools. You three tools. You're foolish in thinking about God and his rules. Your wicked plea passive, when what are Love's rules? To map out a progress? You fools, you are fools."

Then bleeding, it stopped. It stopped on a dime, just like time, for the eagle had run out of blood and of rhyme. Then dying the bird, along with the Model, fell from the cliffs, through air it did tumble, its wings are now useless, its feathers are soaked, heedless of time and its clench on the fools.

Next the crow, not yet dead, landed upon the Cartographer's head, and sang his own song. Thus he sang:

"Which of you fools, which I will choose, to be the most foolish, so foolishly used? The Mapmaker's progress, still hidden though true, cannot be most foolish, his purpose, it grew. A bird needs no map, for as the crow flies, the distance is constant, persistent realized, yet Artists and Models, when they do travel, shall use the map hidden, the map they will follow. The Artist is patient, he takes his sweet time in carving the cliffs, the art is his climb, steady and slow and slow going he is. No, not the most foolish, the Artist he lives. The Model, the body, he's the most stupid. The flesh and the bones of the person, the cupid, the lover he is, the tool of the Artist, and frozen he was before time, its catharsis. He is most foolish, the Model, he dies. Locked in a pose, in a stance, in a trance, waiting for predator time with its lance to gouge through his throat, to behead the eagle, for love is the tool, the insect, the beetle."

The crow in a caw, in a flutter takes off and flies to his perch, an oak tree aloft. He watches the seagull, who in turn landed on the Cartographer's head, red with blood from the eagle.

The seagull sang his song next, the Model still frozen in death's drowning clench.

"Poor Model, he's drowning, how foolish is he? How can he be foolish, he fell to the sea. The map of love drawn, the Cartographer's game, the picture the portrait the painting displayed, yes beauty there is in both Artist and map, yet the portrait itself, it oozes its sap, the blood of love drowning, poor Model, the tool of the Artist who's drawing the still life, Love's rule, draw again, dear Cartographer, sketch the rain of love true, for time starts again while all these thoughts brew."

Eyes

Deep in the blue roaring tide, the Model, the Love, battles Death. For if Love
dies, no map can be drawn except to Death itself, and no portrait of beauty
shall sit on the shelf.
The wisdom of the three birds echo in the ears of the three fools.
The Artist and Cartographer look down the cliffs to watch the struggle
between.
Swimming fish wait for food, their love, their habit. Fish swim and eat. The
bait, the Model, the Love, drowns. The ocean's oracle, in lies it lies,
surrounding boisterously, tossing and turning the Model side to side. Towards
the rocks the tide carries the Love, in contradiction it buries the tarrying parry,
the struggle between the water and body.
Waiting and watching for saltwater death, the fish eat the eagle. Feathers
fetched fingers filing fretted denial, the shirt that was changed shows catchers
deprival, deriving the Love, the Model, the spiral, the eggs stay unhatched.
Without truth, there is no truth. Without Love, there is no love. Without a
map, there is no following. Create the truth with love, draw the map, follow it.
Without sun and rain, flowers stay unbloomed and unblossomed. Who was
the most foolish? The Model, yes, the love itself, to believe that beauty will sit
on the shelf. The seagull, the lover, it bothersome sings and brings nothing but
repetitive circles on wings. The pacing crow confides wisely, stomp out all the
love, for worship of God is not peace like a dove. The eagle, still headless, its
flesh torn to bits by brainless and thoughtless hunger from fish. The fish eat
the eagle. The fish eat the Model. The cupid drowns in the false ocean,
drowns in the foolishness of the Artist and the Cartographer, and drowns in his
own stupidity. The seagull is joined by hundreds of others who perch on the
corpse and devour the Lover.
The sharks come swiftly, following the scent of blood on the tide. The fish eat
the Love. The sharks eat the fish. The seagulls escape with Love in their
stomachs. They escape the razor teeth of the sharks, fly high upon the cliffs,
and draw circles with their wings. The seagulls continue to squawk
annoyingly. Sing love harshly, birds. The crow lives and waits. Two more
fools still live.
Watching the gory destruction of Love, the Artist turns to the Cartographer.
"What now shall we draw, what map can you make, when purpose itself was

eaten like cake?"
The Artist, he painted a portrait of Love.
The Cartographer drew what he could from above.
The Model was left to fly in the stomachs of annoying seagulls.

So

Black as night bites trite insightful, quite delightful light in rightful parody, the kite fell like a rarity is found to tell a snare, you see, the glee of needing pairs to be a person, me. Without light there is no dark, without timing there is no spark, without ears one cannot listen, without tears no criers glisten. Without fear, no bravery true and without truth a lie must do.

Truth is red when it is said, to lie in green would deny the dead, for what is true when the end must come, when love spins circles, woven, spun. Yes, if it stops flying or slows the run then lie love does, and hate will come like stagnant breeze, no, love is active, passive love shoves out a massive valid contradiction racket, gives in to lies told through love plastic. In my ears and out my mouth this does and will till the end comes, the harvest krill. To have peace, war must end. Obvious equations rend the battle fruitless, true, it's fruitless. Which gives first? Love or Love? Those sentenced are guilty until freed. Those innocent are innocent whether sentenced or not. Love stands firm, and so does Love. Nobody can be anyone until someone becomes them. Everybody could be guilty of anything. Anybody could be anyone. Actions are what humanity relies on. Words will forever be only words.

Noir digested voices in the head of thoughts the choice is not a choice, you see when all we see are chairs and teething wrinkled glares to flee. Drilled to the wall in darkness gives the light its time to focus, splinters aspens in psychotic white hypnotic caught it, shot it.

The Cartographer fell from the clouds with the rain, gravity naming his excellent game, blaming the sky for all of the pain in mapping the progress he barely could tame. The trail's consistent but winding and sheer, the crooked persistent eaves of the nearing arrival of ground, of sleep coming sound, round earth and its founding foundation, its hound.

The Model, The Love, in circles it spun around the raindrops, the clouds hide the sun. Plummet the mapmaker splashes on gunshots one two three four gunshots, they're hard to ignore. The shore of the cliffs the Artist, he sits, in patience he paints and painted the nation, the army of Love, the sharks and the fish, the Seagull squawks lonely and sings its own wish.

Thus he sang.

You

"Artist, you effortless shit of the earth, how can you believe you have any worth? What are you drawing but blood over blood? The ruddy confusal of food between cud?"

The Artist expecting an answer as well, a lesson to learn from the Seagull, from Hell, continued his art in respectful silence, miles above the sea and its violence.

The Cartographer groaned, frightened he moaned, toning the honed piece of map he was loaned. Where has he been now.

The Crow as he watched the scene spoke again. He croaked in his smoker's voice cloaking the den.

Thus he sang.

"Two fools yet alive, in body, in mind, yet living the third still flies with his kind, two fools still drawing and painting and flying so which one dies first, with death who will bind? The Artist he's still, he is watching the scene, his feet on the ground, his detail is keen. The Cartographer falls, from black clouds he still plummets, running his brain over places and sonnets, caught between black sky and ground still suspended and bending the will of the rain his art mended the movement of mind, of body and life, of showing the pathways of Hell and its strife. The Artist, it's true, less foolish is he, yet rely he still does on Cartographer's bravery. But foolish and doomed the Mapmaker plummets to death on the rocks, on the cliff's very summit."

Time didn't stop. Neither did death.

The Cartographer's head explodes in a breath.

Two fools are now dead, The Artist remains, taking his time in perfecting his pain.

The Crow he sat still. The Seagull, he circles. The Eagle, still lifeless. Pacing with the fish and the sharks.

Joining the Crow on the branch in the rain, the Owl and the Hummingbird enter the game.

See

Red eye encompassed in photo third month it's the Artist who lives now in bird's eye view trump. Let mercury settle in nettle, the kettle now boils its oil in foiling the toil, see mercury now, the wings on the ankles in Hermes the power of messaging fern thieves. The cherry tree leaves white in lavender spite, obscuring the sight of the reader's politeness, retract the past as anyone does, buzz the natural gas the alarming new tug of craft shattering glass in Saturn, the pattern derives of its past now what matters is splattered. Eat dirt donkey shadow, the meadow is ready to carve with a bread knife, as ready the eddy will jetty with petty thoughts over and over the basil knots loan her: Ideas. Ideas, they're as constant as sunlight, as sure as the moon in night blankets the earth tight. Ideas. They're thoughts and they're fleeting perhaps, yet spring comes when winter's egg cracks and green grass runs idea, idea, until the end of a life. Ideas from birth to the death, till bright lights insert themselves angrily, peacefully, prodigy pressing the odyssey to sleep in a coffin, see: Who is that talking inside of our brains? We say what we choose, we choose what to say, we keep to ourselves what we decide is not playing the role of our person, our character sure, we shear our words edited like brushing out fur in a dog's hide our thoughts lie in minds we are stuck. Can we think out of character? If so, our luck in being a person has run its due course. No, our thoughts are ourselves, a horse is remorse, and force is what keeps thoughts at bay like a porcelain drug, every man, every woman is tied to a beacon, a lighthouse, a lie to prescribe them into believing they are who they are, we are who we are because ideas in brains round the world do run far. To be taught by a fool hardly sounds kind, but the Artist has words to place in your mind. We think in our head. Do we choose what to think? If so, we are choosing what not to think, think: A man sees an object, hears the word of the thought, pops into his brain as he walks down the block. The object is passed, the word it remains in his mind it is fast as his thinking is played by the object itself, it sits on the shelf of his mind, he decides what to do with that rhyme. The object stirs memory, something long lost, a memory of choosing to pay a dear cost, the choice was before him, he chose and he paid, now the memory of paying remains thought displayed. Does he choose to remember? Or was it a choice? If he didn't so choose then what chose for the voice in his head to remember? Was it himself? Who else could it be? This is not mental health, or is it, you see? REACTION.

An argument, vision, a fight between two. A woman, a man, the fight it is due. They vocalize sides, one on one their horse rides like the tide their tongues twist, back and forth their peace hides. Simple that is, a character takes, a side against thoughts another replaced in that other's own brain. Two sides, yes two sides. Valid is the fight when characters collide.

Now again, take a thought, you think it you will. Shrill that thought is, and not who you will yourself to be true, you'd never say you would be quite like that thought, that thought which was due. A thought caused that thought, emotion reacts. Stacking the thoughts and emotions like plaques on your wall, your imagined house of the mind, our thoughts are ourselves, so now let's unwind:

Truth

We choose who we are with our actions. We preach who we are with our words. When regret ties us down, regret of an action or word, what do we regret? Regret of being out of character? Or regret of being the character we were in? Nobody ever can really know who they are. We are stuck in time. All we have of ourselves is memories. In essence, we are all dead, our life is the past.

Before we make a choice, a choice has to be there. To make a choice, one must decide. If the decision itself is difficult, yes, the process of choosing is best to be made in quiet deduction inside the chooser's brain. This or that? The chooser weighs both sides carefully, which side is me? You see, questioning air inside one's own void, the mind's endless cosmos, to decide a decision goes: it's cons and it's pros show the person's becoming, which side is the character I choose in ruling, in running, pursuing? A day to day process, as death wraps its arms in relaxing embrace, the end of the charm. We choose all day long to be who we are, the choices are memories of who we chose to be.

To fight against your own thoughts is to fight yourself. This can lead to discontent with the self. To resist the battle of fighting your own thoughts is refusing to become. We are all in a constant state of becoming. If we refuse to become, we become stagnant. This leads to discontent with other people's selves. Our characters become us instead of us becoming the character we desire.

Everyone desires Love.

The Hummingbird watches the Artist making his marks on the paper, his heart wished the strokes of a brush brings the Hummingbird's words, rushed to the Artist's ears happily heard.

Thus he sang.

"You foolish young Artist, it's hard to ignore the shore laps in red, the fish swim with Love. The Seagull above spins its circles, so cover your head, warm your feet, hear the beat of my wings and be happily dead while the ocean blue sings. You're painting of Love and The Model has color, the time spent in bathing the pages another, another you paint the sketch has been drawn, so sleep in sweet death for Love still lives on."

The Owl leaped up from his perch on the branch.

Thus he sang.

"Let him be, he is young, he is passionate true, he's tried and he's trying to prove his art through a deliberate addiction to futile approval of seeing in his eyes the art as perfected. Don't goad him with lies to bring his demise, don't surprise his hand steady with fluttering sighs sung in happy tone tarries, the Love he shows buys The Cartographer's corpse its own time and own rhyme, so let him be young, for in passion he flies."

The Seagull swept his circles around the Artist's head.

The Crow in his turn sang his song, the notes burn.

Now

Thus he sang.

"The Artist works hard, for long has he toiled, the painting's not finished but royal in color, still the fool works and foolish is he, for you see he won't finish the art, that's his fee. Forever and ever the Artist will sit and paint circles and lines with the color he picks. Too foolish is this, his song is sung, so sadly it's time for him to be hung."

The rope rounded tightly around his poor neck, the Artist pushed off of the cliff, like a wreck he did fall, dying so quickly with legs dangled dead and lifeless and sickly. The four birds, now sitting on the branch on the tree meet the dying with comments, the tale's ending fee.

The Seagull:

"Pre-Agincourt hanging, spectacular so, the Judas was hung, art's truth can now show."

The Crow:

"Sam Hall went a swinging, he knew death was bringing the necessity ringing to Highwayman choke. Snap the neck of the Highwayman, and sway side to side, the right way to die to man is realized."

The Hummingbird:

"Guy Fawkes, that bravery is sick indeed yes, what purpose was there except freedom at best?"

The Owl:

"I've seen this before, a bridge not too far, Owl Creek they may call it, occurrence that bars the dead man was dying in seconds he died, and in his death art was barely realized. A rush to the head, the rope may have snapped, living or dead, escape plan did hatch. He died there perhaps, yet think again, wait, does the Basterd Apache narrow escape?"

The Hummingbird:

"On a lighter note, Crow, or wise Owl, please tell, the date today what is the date now in Hell?"

The Crow:

"May 17th."

The Seagull:

"What a day, what day, a day of all days, to "die" to the "world," in a glorious blaze."

PART IV: The Forgiven Insanity

Theorem IV

The Dead seek to devour The Living.

whereas: The Dead fear The Living for The Living have the power of resurrection, instilling life and subsequently Desire, which results in Suffering.

whereas: Death is the brother of a calm entropy, swallowing a piece of all that it touches within every energy interaction between The Living and The Dead.

whereas: The Dead do not Desire, instead it is the instinct of the beast that drives them.

whereas: When The Dead devours The Living, The Dead has The Living inside them and The Living has The Dead surrounding them.

    1) Why is it The Dead's instinct to have The Living inside of them? It gives the illusion of Life without the Truth of Desire.

    2) Why is it The Dead's instinct to surround The Living? It is a vicarious attempt to kill both Desire and Suffering.

The Dead seek to devour The Living.

1- I am so Sick

Running tired, soliloquy grounded and escaped, this new tear gas explodes my brain. I am nobody. I have no secrets to reveal, I am naked and wandering the cliffs of cataclysmic delirium, approachable, yes, but still lost within waves of particle recognition. Laughable lingering tries to vivify a pressing issue, a tall viewed mutation from xylophone discovery, discovery due, discovery hateful, discovery of love and peace and forgiveness dripping tastefully and tired, still running, still sweating like a fox looking for the birdhouse, like the bird looking for the tree, like the tree looking for the sun, like the sad sun shining as it warms those around it. Break me down, insert your voice into my brain, use me like a morphing tool or a shot of morphine boiled into the skin and breaking and entering casually and often, delayed with dogma and the consistent idea of growing up. Don't go, please, don't go, the oxen still have plowing to do, the raven calls through the gorgeous night and the seagull swims and dives and mourns the moon as the wolfhound wanders my subconscious, trying so hard to break its own fall with freedom, its cranium delivered like a package to an American. This skull has emotion still, take pity, and show it how to die. There are a million directions and a million signs pointing in each one, and to follow any is pursuit of none. My words spill unknowingly, I speak no language, I speak none at all, I lie upon the dew-dripped ground waiting for beautiful night to pass into beautiful morning. I cannot retract, there is no catharsis except for thought, that double-edged sword that slices my throat constantly with a split self, one that cannot run from the darkness into the sun or sprint headlong heedless into the dark, ignoring the blue sky and calling it dull, fatherless, redundant, for the stars call my name and I must go but I don't know where or when or why or how and the questions dissolve me like a rotting deer, shot by an arrow and dead and forgotten, slow to decompose and reeking of mighty death. Pollen canopy dovetailed the founder's bones, crusted into oblivion red and black, the color disruption, revealed to few and desired by many. Clustered, the orca swims swiftly North, eventual with faith and replacing garden talk with eulogies of the noun. Plastic bottles break solid, frozen in a glare of the solar system, wallowing through abyssal dreams and nightmares and the life awake, all valid, all separate, all hellish. The hand falls from the sky, the sun falls behind the moon, buildings fall into the icy lake, splintered and corrupted and mutilated and dreary and tedious and valued at nothing by those who understand nothing.

2- I am so Hurt

Borders broken delay the innocuous revealings, the slender incarnate hooves
yellow with astrology, plankton migrating with the wind and catastrophes
inaugurated build a swaying tower, shifting like blankets upon a bed of
sapphires, down to the hellish beyond and sinking fast, quickly, stammered
like a parrot who has had one too many cigarettes to behold, one too many
ammonia capsules dissolved upon his tender trachea, meager, so meager,
lifting its head from death to look beyond the stone, beyond the holy rock
symbolizing nothing except whatever the viewer views to be necessary. This
is not a game, this is not a child running in a playground, shouting the
swindlers and the evasions putrid, cannonballing the calm entropy dusk vapor
bold and beauteous and old, so old, so eager to die in a discarded box of nails
and screws and deadly viper fangs dripping with lead from Satan's cuffs, from
his disembodied voice leading all those who organize choking, who placate
mystery, who eat clams on a Sunday afternoon after holy church shrouded in a
mist of forgiveness, who rock and sway beneath willow wasps and vulture
head ages, who roll with heavy eyelids upon beds bare and empty and lonely,
who experience love in a nighttime of sexual fantasies lived out to the fullest
with a single hand and a solitary brain, who try to break the mold before the
substance has dried frozen and fallen in our eyes, who try to canonize hope
into something ethereal and belonging and claustrophobic always entrenched
and mutilated, who quilt carefully and methodically as sunshine smells single
out the farmer's corpse by dawn, who wrench away ostrich feathers from the
hands of the chieftain of Sabbath immobilized, who eagerly underestimate
time and the expensive throne that sits upon the king himself, who rally upon
cries of the poor and the rich and those who cannot be either although wanting
to be both whichever is convenient at the time, who trust in horns and trumpets
heralding the second and third and fourth and fifth comings, who yell often
and ornery, who utilize branches like seeds and seeds like branches, who incite
hooks to the fish gum and the worm gut, who ovulate expensive jewelry and
wonder why nobody cares, who prescribe medications for things that ail all,
who assess the donkey shadow and call it wise, who shiver tenderly at each
word bludgeoned upon the brain also so tender, who drape expensive columns
at midday like an iconoclast of firm denial, who foam at the mouth every time
somebody disagrees with them, who goad frogs into crossing the alligator

marsh on a catfish morning, who hold on so tightly to nothing and cry when it slips through their fingers, who jump ecstatically too often to let others believe in their ecstasy, who kill without killing until they die without dying, who lock doors to keep in the harshest of elements. Lead us, for we are lost.

3- I am so Confused

And yet the clock ticks, verily sound and clacking like a train tantrum, bold and voluptuous and near, the faithful hound builds a startling new earth, a new continuum bladed and vanished upon the starry night beheld as a mystery due, mystery final, mystery mysterious and holy and upon the shrouded temple of crested mountains covered in ferns and lilacs, lowly hanging and lorded upon a tall tree of nothing. There is always hope because there might as well be. Hope is a choice, hope is not given or taken but chosen upon the brain of those who deem its power to be its own braid, its own hair falling upon shoulders and backs scarred by whips of the loving. This dawn is itself and nothing more, it has no mind, it has no feeding tentacles wrapped in the octopi incarnation, the dew ink hiding all that there is left, which is nothing more than the endless quiet. These rivers will flow until the end, these waves will lap upon the shore of the forgiven and understood by minds that cannot understand, and this boat rocks gently upon the tide. Nothing is undone when nothing exists. And so we wander the ghoulish setting, the cliffs of the hungry decided in a lapping tongue, in a pair of eyes that melts the snow and shatters the mind of those it sees and invades all privacy without meaning to. Catastrophe is a concept, death is a concept, life is a choice and we all choose without knowing we do, welded upon a metal without vanity and a golden band worn around the eyebrows, isolated, yes, but willing upon all the moon's bought solidifications, the lunar goddess immobile yet loving and accepting of the howling and the roaring and the shouting from its own perfect chaos, brutality of the soul vapid but also willing as the moon, as the stars lifted beyond the curtain that was ripped in half and evaded into an orchestra, a symphony of soulless ivory veering to the north as Apollo warms this world and sends the geese sprinting towards its sheer incapabilities.

4- I am so Stoic

Let my earnesty be my map, let the stories slide into something tangible, let me escape into the great unknown knowingly and unperturbed, the beautiful eagle soaring above hills and plains and cities and mountains, the crag instigated by glades of aspen and revealed osmosis to the next kind. Let my wings carry me in every direction, a father of columns, a father of rope, a father of hummingbird anguish, nectar infused and ready, slamming upon the table of denial into the seaside bed of forgotten dues. Corruption will follow us forever, always possibilities revert themselves into oranges and apples and other tyrannical fruits that must be ignored and focused upon simultaneously. The clay made crawfish slender instills the hearty orifice, the water tight and seeping into cracks in the leather boat. This will be unto the end, the boat ever sinking, ever plunging into the night of trenches, the masquerade of foolish pride, the fish hatchery involved with nothing but itself and tried and true and false and withered upon complexions gravely mistaken for a mirror, for there is no accurate reflection to follow upon except the map of earnesty, of passionate arrows ignited to castle walls and moats filled with nothing but seedless carp, smoking the sideways train track, wilting upon a twilight of nocturnal blessings awry, redefined according to lyrics and according to song tasteful, broken and moral and honest. The veneer cascades down the hillside, rocks latticing the molecular emotion, the banister of health and mental xenophilia without selection due or denied, desperation in the mind of a werewolf who has been taught to heel and sit quietly and patiently until the wilderness overcomes his shadow and blows everything into the water and out of proportion. Caustic, the rust immobile confiscates a mitigated response, for what is this zoo? Who are these animals surrounding, moving betwixt and between the temple's tapestry enveloping, for the similarities are stark and the differences robust. Blossom, my child. Blossom unto oblivion, the hymn musicality sounding off like a siren holding the treasure close to her human breast, gravely inspired and eagerly earnest as well. Tie me to the mast, let me hear the song of freedom while my last breath is choked from my shallow lungs, my private immunity cataclysmic into a breaking feather, a beaten wing of blushing modesty, a humility beguiled into a smaller set of notes, the chromatic scale now scolded as too hearty, too knowing, too pretentious upon the jazz head volumized and placated. This place is itself and nothing more, and to love it means to love its wanderers, its ants scattered and worker bees brave and bold, swarming to sting the mind of the unholy until death wraps its loving embrace and reasons with itself. The idol is not real. The mantra itself is fake, there is no beard worth remembering or hair gray worth forgetting, so, in quiet, be still, child, and breath your last. This was never your war, your planet pursuing itself at breakneck speed, your opium den infested with rats, your church infested with forgiveness, your garden infested with rose bushes blossoming, blossoming like you, child, in all your fear and all your confusion and all your courage withheld because it is indeed not yours. It belongs to the animals clamouring for your will, it belongs to the beasts wandering the halls of your subconscious, dangerous and calm. Try to have peace, welcome serenity, for there is no battle. There are no casualties, no horses impaled upon stakes protruding from the brain of the beloved. There is no deciding judge harkening you to believe in nothing or everything or anything possible. This is a facade, no matter what end it reaches, no matter what vestitude marks the fortuitous blinking of eyes demure and warlike, angry and hopeful, honest and evading all truth at all costs at all times. The porcelain hound is broken, do not pick up the pieces, instead comb your black mane and lift the young unto sky and sea and air, so tight, so thick and heavy and invisible. The next is not something you need to know, the future is itself and never reaches us, the past is an idea that should not torture you so, forgive yourself and open your arms to the heaven that is on earth, the hell that is in the mind, the union that commutes with the brethren of forgotten fathers and mothers, opening the valve of hinderance and reigns tied strongly to the arm of those who are weak. Extend your mind to the vast above, the sky that rockets our feeble brain to the atmosphere of music, the music of eyes, the eyes of lust, and the lust of the forgiven and given unto and broken by beauty itself, calm, so calm and peaceful in its passing. Revisit the kingship, the matriarchy holy and set upon at the right hand of God and the left hand of Satan and the feet of those who run in faith to the veracity of a finish line founded upon the freedom from guilt and the freedom from chains tied to the tongue and retina. The ivory tower concludes with nothing, nothing is given and nothing is taken away and hope remains true, tried and fiery and pouring upon the altar of a wedding dress, of a veil to be brushed away like a tear of joy, dripping down the cheek upon the ending of a story, of a conflict and confusion, of an eagle soaring South with winter, leading the friendly geese and following its beard intact and aged and springing from rocks struck by a staff of mindless wind.

5- I am so Broken

Can there be an end, for what happens when this motion stops, when the world quits spinning in all its splendor, when the volcanoes erupt sending gaseous poison into the lungs of the aged and young and ready, when the earth shakes upon the arrival of giants, lumbering behemoths crushing the wooden huts and the tiny snakeskin charms, childish and perfect, evolved and evolving, redefined in a mistaken hue, a shade too hopeful to be true and too true to have any hope in survival? Break this chain with me, be my anvil, my hammer, my map to myself and to heaven above in a trebuchet launching across canyons of whispered glory, elevated and prudent to the disguise, the mask honest and showing the face itself and hardly a mask save for the smile, the pearls leading contentment to the open gates of God, ivory and old and exquisite, treacherous to many and precious to all, guided to a glittering sphere that we call home. All of us, yes, all of us, for there is only one you and I, there is only one them and us, there is a we that escapes into the clouds on fire wings and an immortal pegasus kind to us all, cathartic in its travel, teaching the animal in my brain to keep moving, for the end is not an end, it is the connection of a new circle, one of Icarus forgotten, one of Odin and his spear and his loyal wolf calm and dangerous and careful to not frighten its tender cubs as they roll in the long grass, in the wheat fields awry, amongst ferns twelve feet tall and the ant sequoia. Invite this course, this penchant for frivolity and joyous solitude and camaraderie ancient to the stories before, sliding through the serpent immaculate and cleansed, eating away the longing lodged between these hollow ears, for this ugliness does not last. It is finite, it is unreal, it is a shadow in the morning. So climb, dear sun. Climb, my moon goddess beautiful and brave and bold and precious to us all, so many, every character pouring onto this page as the light and the dark agree, they do not need to be separate for they are themselves unto each other, they give each other the respect that flakes down the mountain, dribbling off the chin of a toddler, lapping up through the tongue of a housecat fat and happy and quiet and sleeping. Be free, shadow, and drift upon the winged waves vicarious, march to the beat of the daffodil drum, the lily is now open and tried and found wanting nothing, needing nothing, desiring only wisdom and clarity and contentment in being a flower. The wilderness is ever there, ever waiting for our tattered bare feet to trod, to seep among the sand crystals and sing the revealings given upon the hand of the meter, the honey harvest, vouched and stable in all its terror, in all its confusion forgiven and given time and proceeding with careful reluctance, the funnel cloud now dropping from the heights and lifting instigations to possibilities endless upon thought and singular in action, the duality given heed as the last living tortoise on earth crosses the line. Open. Open these arms to embrace the sickle. Give back to the earth with happiness and guarded calm and quiet, closed lips. Find comfort in the idea of comfort, find the harness and the saddle and the reins held tightly with the thought of bare thread and water washing upon red sand, proceeding to the next phase, the next duty, a challenge of pain and a challenge of growth and a challenge of war against seeping arrogance that crawls across the hallway floor towards clocks grandfathered and icy, that inches its way nearer and nearer to the color of the void, the abyssal circumference of the global jugular, the panic of the cage that will not open and the chain that will forever be shackled to these pupils, understood and at rest with a wary eye.

6- I am so Lost

So the pervasive unknown prunes my brain, a lion pacing through the unsheltered Savannah, ignoring columbine corruption, rendered musical numerals, calling the equations to a reckoning tried and true and ridiculous in nature, natural nuances building the next and the next until walking itself is called green, until the pacing mane veers West and extraneous, the shadow on a painted wall shifting, bubbling like Roman candles and popping as teeth in a bout of metal poles swinging also West, always West, young and old meeting in the middle to placate each other and find themselves to be naked, always West, softly shouldered upon locks of lost and found love. Until the dawn wakens, until those roads slide into the snakeskin shivered amongst rocks and woods and threads within the loom regarded lonely and laughing, until the wolf finds night once again and glorifies Artemis tide, until the stars fall upon hair ties used to oblivious beauty, until stairs that go both up and down are flatlined and curvaceous, until the tile floor breaks upon boulders of sapphire instruction, jeweled denial seeping once again from the mind's ugly encampments on cliffs of creatures not knowing each other and feeding upon the mind of selection and guiding the young to a beyond of safe euthanasia and molding the song possible and pruned, vivacious and erect through symbolism massive and minute, until the eagle itself finds its lamb, its tiny tongue slandering nothing at all and owning itself and the tongues around it through pure volumes outdated and outnumbered and outside the fence of the known and safe, until trees build a causeway throughout the rocks true and labored luxuriously through a dynasty creation and the son of a trivial injection in the wrists and eyes, acid blooming throughout brains tender and brave and confused precarious, morphing the spring to a father of night, of wind howling through city gutters and creeks of the canopy incarcerated by the wind itself and through the pupil fortitude, the idea of fish swimming West, always West, through a sea of peace and war and the swaying between the two, until rabbits hide their trails and the conversations leak indifference from a whaler of wondrous unity isolated as ice roads linger in a dew of humming bluebirds sitting amongst madmen that yell at nothing and whisper at everything that listens or doesn't listen, lost in a haze of dots and connections and patterns of indescribable terror and beauty and laughter and anguish and splintered ingenuity, until the game is over and there is no winner and no loser and nothing but white flags waved, this mind will run in caustic circles, cauterizing a wound until more blood seeps West, always West, all land West now holy and understood as an elephant visiting the gravestone of its fathers and mothers and sisters and aged brothers horned and decomposed by symphonic tethers welded to egotistical quivers sand filled, arrowless, infantile and trapped. The child is lost. The elder is lost. The wilderness calls their name and they answer through sheer progress, through animalistic endeavors of autumn, of spring and winter, of summer glad and gated and profane. Unraveling scarves envelope each other, the gray hair withered upon a tree of infused anger, of bitterness biting and tall, of a saw of blood dripped privation in the thousands, in the millions upon clamoring wills and clamoring denial and quiet humiliation, the memories goaded upon a thorough mastication, the slithered cud squelching between teeth and between minds of the young and old and between ferns of fathers, ferns of death rocks holy, ferns of desire that breaks the heart as it always does as the eagle flies to the Western nest, always West, always dangerous on precipices worthy of kingship, worthwhile in their loneliness and worth nothing to those who care about nothing. This mind is dizzy. Its tornado swirls of hallucinogenic arguments ancient build the mushroom belief, the belief that breaks all knowledge and destroys any other belief including itself, the borders hinged and escapism of ivory luck ludicrous instills the wild lounge, the pipe smoking cindered to incapable delay, to a truth of canary delight and badger alleviation and of the secondhand heron, slyly waiting for fortune's fish to linger beneath pinpoint legs of God's brain and God's hand and God's hatred broken by God's love of lust for life, for death, for the union of the broken and the separation of statehood and a flag waved forever.

7- I am so Tired

Irregular vulgarities construe the passive verbatim, the next kind evolved to an eyeball of enchantment, a wrist of poems verbalized within the throat and ear, a whale longing to move with the tired wind always entrenched within vocabularies of dead musical notes, flatlined and unstable, the alarm sounding off like church bells to show a new morning of cemetery expulsion, a nothing of tapestries and a painting that holds every idea that has ever bludgeoned the brain of any inventor, tired, so tired, so hidden amongst pinion wings and rock guides indifferent, the heights still climbing themselves to reach clouds of rubble, of hand grenades inert and wild and foolish, exploding the adderall with a complex of delusions of grandeur, psychosis permeating the senses as senseless slaughter reigns supreme in the vermin mind of a poet who has died and been born again and died once more, withholding no locked verbs, beheld and beholden by damaged ships torn asunder by seas of noteworthy weakness of pollen dripped upon ladle sprites and utilitarian specters given unto themselves in a bloom of night, in a bloom of terror, in a bloom of a battle that was lost before it was started, lost from both sides as waves crash upon the shipwrecked shoreline, seals infesting the wooden rafters as the sailor corpses plunge into a ragged tatter-torn holiday that brings about no change, that is symbolic for nothing except itself, that shifts the memories cold upon the Sunday morning stark naked and starving from the cicatrix of slender incarceration, from prison cell to prison cell the spirit leaps, languishing in chains of the mind, in chains of the cavern cold, the dream fatigue cat-like upon a yoke of weather worn indecisiveness, prancing amongst the insects like a king crowned by himself and given fealty by no creature, so, in comfort, fall. Fall down the water sliding off rock, sideways upon the mountain to a crevice of nocturnal delight into trout homes of harkened productivity, fall off the parapets into the shifting moat, dancing with the crocodiles lunging from lilypad to ornery lilypad, the cocaine catfish playfully mutating into lions of pacing danger, biting the tongue of aggression until blood seeps upon the inside-out shirt of undignified glory. Illusion packed like a chicken lead to the slaughterhouse, useless wings and quiet clucking, becoming meat for those who don't really need food at all except for the alleviation of boredom and sadness and health. Guarded initiations entrust the game to the padded walls, the white cage closing in around the hummingbird, swallowing its brain and spitting out the bones of creativity on top of the rug of the privileged, the angry, the hopeful and lead, the golden band disintegrates and nobody cares to notice, the fallen are not remembered except by those who killed them, the living are forgotten too except by the living themselves, and the dead that are raised bring the Hell to body, Hell to mind, Hell to soul in a forever of anguish, wallowing in intrepid follicles forgotten as a promise, as a soldier of luck that has fallen to the grave of luck, as a bear who has discovered the honeycomb also discovers the horde of bees that are the size of bears, angry and honest and right in their thinking, the catacombs spent like the dollar of a mogul disguised as a different mogul, one wanting not the money but only what the money can bring: hate, hate, feverish hate. So revel, my child, in confusion lost and found and discarded and picked up again, revel and become yourself, your tried and true nature spotless and spotted, revel and begin again, for we are always at the beginning and always at the end and never, never in the middle, degraded until forever and instilled beyond whiskey breath and cannabis rebuttal and productions mixed with wine on a friday afternoon, giving heaven a second shot, a thief of boyhood charms and envelopes stamped to a number massive as the given unto could be endless and may not be existing at all.

8- I am so Human

It doesn't matter. It's the worship of self, it's enchantment of the ego that builds this eye, this flame retina piercing my skin with its angry gaze, stripping me of my peace and my power over paranoia. It doesn't matter, and the hummingbird will once again be free to find its honey nectar, it's ripe fruit blooming like lotus position progress, its prescriptions of anatomy and biology and chemistry beautiful and wary and constant, giving no ground and receiving nothing in return because indeed, child, it doesn't matter. This cloak, this hellish sunspot vacant and burning, this beaten mask burgeoning from the soul of delusional persecution will once again find rest, not in heaven, but in earthly care, not in receiving the West, but in pursuing it and, in due time, finding it in all it's glory and peace and lovely radiance shining about the stars of warriors who have fallen for a cause and risen for the same cause just to fall once again, fighting a war that nobody sees or hears or cares about, lodged within the pines of a forest that breathes, that talks and walks with those who care for it, fathering particle dust encrusted into the obvious answer, the answer that is coming slowly, carefully and thoughtfully, watching itself delayed like a flower who waits for the sunshine to show its beauty or an eagle that is flying too high for anyone to make out its form. The lion roams, yes, roams and wails in the night alone, so alone, but the pride is nearing and caring and looking for the next oath, the next volumes to date and organize, the sphere of the apple hanging from the tree in a constant, careful, becoming the savior of the self and nobody else and becoming so through the others, through caring and respecting and mutual enthusiasm for life in all its awe, in all its power, given unto death as a friend of judgement, given unto death as a father of night, given unto death as a shadow that frees itself from the bondage ankles and scatters the molecules into a forever of theatrical revelry. It does not and will not matter, so let go, and become the wolf that you are, longing for a black sky that falls upon the earth in cloudless sound, that blankets the rotund scrupulosity in an idea of monstrous warmth, in an idea of vivid motion blind and playing perfectly in the eyes of the saved, in an idea of heaven that is not perfect but exists because it sounds better than Hell. The journey is not closing and that is still beautiful. On the wolf will walk, finding the pack to be loving and nurturing and wild in all its terror, in a canyon of wetted knives inaugurating, polishing the silky tapestry as to not build a carpet of dust and to remember each battle and learn from each strategy, willful, purposeful with peace, for Hell exists to those that believe in Heaven.

9- I am so Animal

Let me wash away into night, into blackness of thought and the leviathan that wakes within eyes, into the waves of the deep desired by orca fin and dolphin whistle. Let me dive into the caverns of musical time, the matriarchal involvement penniless and proud, prying my fingers off parchment to give another a chance, to give each character a say as they speak to each other and argue and baffle the brain god deluded. There are a thousand of me, a thousand thousands, and cannonball misconstruing confides the lumber of the lost innocuous, the glasses fit to deliver a dialogue of tantrum masculinity, of femininity love, of androgynous wandering through mental scapes and blankets of masts cracked and caving, created by dusk and growing each night into a flower of the howl, of the hair standing straight and on edge in wary delight, each blood cell a vanished scale crawling through arpeggios of disguised ambiguity and archipelagos of sand white and turquoise-teethed waters. Nautical allusions evaluate the sperm whale, the ridged elevator of ridiculous oaths from years before plummets with the wind from above into the depths of hydrogen trenches queued and corrupt, clicking the gold pieces together in a clack of reversed enthusiasm, the paid now tired and the employer jubilant as an otter who has found the water's edge and pushed the rowboat into swaying shifts of buoyant zen capitalised upon and reliant. Isolation. The edge of the arrow. The gravestone silent and loyal, the row of ducks marching to doom. Shoot me straight, lift my heart from my ribs and bury me deep below the mantle, the rocks of lying visions, the dreams displaced by a psychotic tremolo, layered in its definition and stacked to the highest of heights. He died of natural causes, his death was natural, spewing nature from his guts into the blood-wrenched grip of titular evolution, spewing nature so terrible, so earthen, so natural. Embody the hurricane, embody the endless quiet that eludes, that covers your tracks in the muddy rain numerals washing upon minds who see through nothing with eyes that blink in fabled rhythm, in a groaning gate of wormhole fruit blossoms through lunatic ego impalement. Embody the beast that lies quietly and patiently, waiting for the ripe darkness to quake and quiver in propelled estrogen evasive, in a wound licked by wolves, cleansed and chilled to the rested bone. Embody the uneasy spirit, the demon wandering from its drug infused lullaby delirium to havens hollow, havens finite, havens of death angel awe and honesty. Embody the specter hindered, reined in by luck and lavish delusions, ludicrous verbs pandered to fit the mold of fungus, of mushroom clouds and clocks of rain tattered sandals, feet to be bloodied upon purpose and sleight of hand. Embody the skull caged hummingbird, dry and toothless, oscillating in respect and vulgarity, its hues illuminating the mind to a road eloquent and inspired by the dead that walk and talk and try, volatile as the wind in March, the belaying of catastrophic immunity and the hands raised in wonder; in eager, peaceful pollution.

10- I am so Loving

Overwhelm me, overwhelm and consume my thoughts in astrological botany pervasive, become the immensity of the single inkling, the wailing of wild canine, the rush of wind running from the tips of the feathered eagle wing. This radioactive heartache stretches from the shallows to the canyons, from the conscious to slithered subconscious. I am the desert, cactus, flower, I am the song unraveled from the rattlesnake singer softly sliding from precipice to dangled precipice. I am the moon, shining upon black and soaking hearts. I am the coyote wandering naked in the springtime deluge, dorsally unknown and prepared for the tumor of any mystical dichotomy. I am the rock silently waiting for wind and water to paint runways upon my sandstone back, aged, hopeful and hopeless simultaneously, circular in dawn and dusk and spherical in the making, giving forgiveness gladly and receiving it and nothing else, a wrecking ball of inhibition hallowed and thermal. I am the black panther hunting and hunted, hiding amongst the bushes blushing with pride and demure agnosticism, holding their thorns as parapets of recognized wonder, the eighth and the ninth and the tenth. I am the quiet owl shifting as shadows in the blackness of illegible thievery, scooping up the hindered rabbit soft, gurgling on choked bones and flesh and blood that gives life as it takes it away. I am the brook, bubbling West and earnest, eager to find lodging within the muddy alleyways, eager, so eager and so loving in its kind watering and nourishment. I am the trail on the ancient map, vivid in color and in causeway, tattered to a bridge of broken promises that have been perpetually patched and forgotten, stark to new exponents and a fraction closer to being simpler. I am the countless grains of sand, there is every formation of crystalline shape within these bones, infinite in its shifting scope and I change, yes, change with the weather as the wind howls like a wolf along the dunes of my ego.

11- I am Dying

Death, answer me. For where am I? Am I lost in the nebulous haze of forgotten insanities, now remembered and shaven like pine residue upon a delicate mind of birthing equations, meandering through space in a boat that sways upon waves a thousand feet high, crashing down with the pouring rain and spinning endlessly upon eagle wing waterspouts? Am I wandering the desert of temptation, clueless on when to bow and what to bow to and how to bow in the first place, an arrow protruding from my bleeding soul, shot by a sprite of sinister ambitions or nymph that redefines beauty in a way that cannot be written or spoken or worded at all, instead given back to the instinct of the animal? Is this wilderness to be my home? Am I to create a lean-to and build a fire to warm these frigid fingers so dainty upon the neck of an unused guitar? Death, answer me. For what am I? Am I beast, animalistic in cause and effect, uniting the birds of the air and fish of the sea and the wandering creatures of the land within a mind of instinct, lead by the devil, my nouns and verbs sent by Hell, a spirit of humanity within the eyes of the animal, longing to break free from this skull and experience the wild terror of a cageless life, a gargoyle of ambiguous mysticism that follows its gut and nothing else, that worships everything as a deity to be respected, all things a single entity of created and creator, bearing unseen power until it itself is destroyed in the flames of sulfuric acid, a monstrosity, a leviathan of love that uses hate as an ally as doom sings with a voice melodious and tender and embracing, uniting the people as stars plummet upon our necks and backs? Death, answer me. For why is this happening?

12- I am Living

The days ring, they pierce my ears steadily, harming my tubes and canals and passageways to the weary mind, the gate black now opening to portray an army of demons, demons of barbaric life between two ears, between two lungs, with two hands upon an incline leading to a boat that holds everyone and everything and every idea that has ever graced the knuckles of the workingman. It is desire that is breaking your heart, festering within wooden hallways of clocks rotund and red, ticking away life as you live in the depressant past and the anxious future, forgetting the pleasure of the present, the table well-fed, the roof that has no leak, the embrace of the loving wrapped tightly around this beastly form. Ingenuity peaks as the psychedelic intensifies, a peak that is broad, yes, broad and long and will last a lifetime among lifetimes, not slandered, no, not slandered or mitigated or slowing in its tantric spin, instead upon the heights, the goat hoof sound in its footing upon the manic cliffs set apart by a choice. This, or that. It is impossible to choose, and when there is no reality, when all realism crumbles down like a castle during siege and its inhabitants slaughtered, when people are no longer entities but thoughts only, when thoughts are no longer thoughts but energy, when energy gives in to entropy dismay and the heavenly clock clicks away at the wormhole sucking in all that was once believed to be believable, this is when God appears. It is not seen or heard. It is not felt or tasted. It simply is, is and will be as this facade lived daily by each thought walking and talking melts into oblivion. It simply is, is and will be as the mask worn by the world is taken off to show no face beneath it. It simply is, is and will be, surrounding, enveloping, imagining this vivid existence that doesn't exist at all.

13- I am Trying

And yet there is still connection. Not connection in words, but in spirit; in the
unspoken. I am surrounded by thoughts who think about me while I ruminate
about these mirrors, this hallway long and horrendous bearing the native
masquerade, the imminent death that you, child, do not fear, that you do not
understand, inhabited by a killer that is a wraith that you have never seen or
heard or tasted or felt but still, throughout the fearless confusion, exists
through faith and nothing else except hope and nothing else except love. For
what is doomed within me? These bones and this flesh? Am I to fall to the
earth in tired sleep, decompose tenderly as food for the insects that mind their
own business and hide without trying to, self-aware and teeming in the dusk of
forgotten woes? Is it this burden upon your back to be lifted in the light of a
new day and the dark of a new night, lifted not through Heaven's eyes or
Hell's left hand but through the ending of a battle that ended because it never
existed in the first place, the story falling throughout the cracks in your mind
as the world's mask slides down showing a face that looks exactly the same as
the mask? Are these eyes leading towards execution, always looking at what
they do not have until the guillotine falls through the roar of a lion, the blind
now able to see but not with eyes, not with retina ridged or the pupil of
ambitions that meet their match in the gladiatorial arena, both sides doomed to
die within a victory of the crowd that loves and cares and doesn't enjoy the
entertainment but is destined to watch the gore spill from emotional caverns
cold and deep and hidden in oceanic trenches far below the crust of the
spinning orb we do not own but love to abuse? Is it your desire that is
doomed, child, your yearning for the ambiguous to become legible in a
language that you understand but were never taught, instead an heirloom of
chemicals that have no name and no home and no purpose other than to be
themselves, in all their swirling hallucinations, the wilderness to be pervasive
and your house on resting rock imbued, on jungle vines swinging with
trembling honor, hitched upon the horse that you ride forward and forward and
forward? Is it my ego that will be buried, no gravestone adorning the dirt that
covers its sickly and unholy form, a doom decided upon by the omnipresent it
and forgotten, laid to rest in order for you to be yourself, child, in all of your
immaturity and longing and idealism while penniless, penniless and happy in

all the spiritual connection from this animal to its caretakers kind? Death awaits us all, as does life in all its splendor.

14- I am

We inch closer, closer to the lion sleeping upon bullets lent to the brain in tender care, the wolf cut to pieces, the eagle wings clipped and the hummingbird caged. The sleep comes, you see it, child, you see its approach and you dread it, you dread the end as you dread all things. Harps play, listen. There is still grass upon this forest floor green and life-giving. The clouds will make their shapes for the rest of the beyond, the ground will lay beneath these tired and bloody feet as it always has and always will. The end is coming, child. Do not fear defeat, for in defeat there is hope for yourself, hope for the emotion of the calling wind, hope for the sounds that emulate off of every singer's tongue. There is hope in the birth of a new soul within you, a forgiven soul of purity cleansed. There is hope in the ocean that sways, rocking the wooden craft you ride so long, so hard, so scared, so tired. There is hope in the bird that rests upon your knuckles, sweetly singing and guiding your movements throughout the heart-breaking game that will not and will never end. There is hope in the trees growing tall and strong and able to withstand the weather that will undoubtedly come, that will shake this world in all its hellish ignorance. There is hope in lilacs wild, wandering amongst insects and mice looking for a home and a haven. There is hope in the honeybee, yes, even in the honeybee. And although you don't believe in this hope, child, this hope believes in you.

Theorem V

Life demands age. Death knows no age.

     whereas: Life counts moments as it moves, rating each one on a scale of Desire.

     whereas: Life renders the process of actualization of Desire into linear progress and the actualization of Desire gives age by the simple moving from pt. A to pt. B.

     whereas: Death is simultaneously old and young, for without actualization the linear progress is connected circularly, at each end, and The Dead transcend age and maturity, a construct of The Living.

Life demands age. Death knows no age.

The sagebrush sprouts, grows, spreads, and burns.
The seed acquires a root.